Heidelberg Travel

Guide 2024

A Day in Heidelberg: Making

the Most of 24 Hours in

Germany's Charming City"

By

Arnfried S. Reinhard

Table of content

Introduction

Welcome to the Heidelberg Travel Guide! Nestled along the serene banks of the Neckar River, Heidelberg is a charming city steeped in history and brimming with cultural treasures.

This guide is your passport to discovering the enchanting blend of medieval architecture, picturesque landscapes, and vibrant local culture that defines Heidelberg.

Join us as we explore the must-visit attractions, savour delectable cuisine, and uncover the unique experiences that make Heidelberg a destination.

Whether you're a history enthusiast, a nature lover, or simply seeking a delightful getaway, let this guide be your companion to unlock the wonders of Heidelberg. Get ready to embark on a journey through cobblestone streets, scenic hills, and centuries-old charm – welcome to Heidelberg!

Chapter One

Overview of Heidelberg

Nestled in the heart of Baden-Württemberg, Germany, Heidelberg stands as a testament to the country's rich history and cultural heritage.

This picturesque city, often hailed as one of the most romantic in Germany, boasts a perfect blend of medieval charm and modern vitality.

Historical Significance

Heidelberg's history dates back to the 5th century, with its crowning jewel being the Heidelberg Castle, perched majestically on the Königstuhl hill.

The castle, a symbol of German Romanticism, has witnessed centuries of triumphs and tribulations, contributing to Heidelberg's unique character.

Architectural Marvels

The Altstadt (Old Town) is a maze of narrow streets with well-preserved Renaissance buildings, charming squares, and historic landmarks. The Karl Theodor Bridge, also known as the Old Bridge, connects the Old Town to the opposite bank of the Neckar River, providing stunning cityscape views.

Academic Hub

Heidelberg is renowned for its prestigious University, founded in 1386, making it the oldest in Germany. The University has been a nurturing ground for numerous Nobel laureates, scholars, and thinkers, adding an intellectual vibrancy to the city.

Cultural Riches

Beyond its academic achievements, Heidelberg offers a vibrant cultural scene. The Philosophers' Walk, a scenic path along the Neckar River, has inspired poets and philosophers for centuries. The city annually hosts various festivals, concerts, and events, celebrating its cultural diversity.

Natural Beauty

Surrounded by lush green hills, Heidelberg provides a stunning backdrop for exploration. The Neckar River weaves its way through the city, offering delightful riverside strolls, and the nearby Odenwald Forest provides ample opportunities for nature enthusiasts.

Modern Amenities

While steeped in history, Heidelberg seamlessly blends tradition with modernity. Cafés, restaurants, and boutiques cater to locals and visitors, creating a dynamic atmosphere. The city's commitment to sustainability and innovation is evident in its eco-friendly initiatives and progressive urban planning.

In essence, Heidelberg is a city where history comes alive, where the old and the new harmonize, inviting travellers to immerse themselves in a captivating journey through time and culture.

Brief History

With its rich tapestry of history, Heidelberg stands as a testament to the passage of time and the resilience of culture. The city's roots trace back to Roman times when it was established as a military outpost. However, it was in the 13th century that Heidelberg truly flourished.

1386, the University of Heidelberg was founded, solidifying the city's status as a centre for academia.

The University was pivotal in shaping Heidelberg into an intellectual hub during the Renaissance. The famous philosopher Marsilius of Inghen and humanist Johann Reuchlin are among the notable figures associated with their early academic prowess.

The jewel in Heidelberg's crown is undoubtedly the Heidelberg Castle, perched majestically on the Königstuhl hill. Construction of the castle began in the 13th century, and it witnessed expansions and renovations over the centuries.

The castle served as the residence for the Palatinate Electors, showcasing the city's significance in the political landscape.The 16th and 17th centuries they brought both prosperity and challenges. Heidelberg became a cultural epicentre with the establishment of the Bibliotheca Palatina, one of Europe's most significant libraries.

Unfortunately, during the Thirty Years' War, the city faced destruction, leaving the castle in ruins. Despite this setback, Heidelberg experienced a cultural revival during the Romantic period, inspiring poets and artists.

Heidelberg's charm extends to its Old Town (Altstadt), where narrow alleys and well-preserved buildings transport visitors back in time.

The Philosophers' Walk, overlooking the city, has hosted renowned intellectuals inspired by its serene ambience.

Today, Heidelberg stands as a blend of its historic past and modern vibrancy. Visitors can traverse its landmark streets, admire the remnants of the castle's grandeur, and bask in the intellectual aura that continues to define this captivating city.

The historical narrative of Heidelberg is not just a tale of bygone eras; it's a living, breathing testament to the enduring spirit of a place that has witnessed centuries unfold within its cobblestone streets.

Why Visit Heidelberg

Heidelberg, a gem in the heart of Germany, beckons travellers with its irresistible allure and multifaceted charm. Here are compelling reasons why Heidelberg deserves a place on your travel itinerary:

Historic Splendor: Heidelberg is synonymous with its iconic castle – a majestic ensemble overlooking the city. The Heidelberg Castle's rich history, dating back to the 13th century, is a testament to the city's medieval grandeur. Visitors can wander through its timeless ruins, immersing themselves in tales of royalty, wars, and romance.

Enchanting Old Town (Altstadt): The cobblestone streets of Heidelberg's Old Town exude medieval charm and vibrant baroque architecture.

Stroll through the Marktplatz, visit the Church of the Holy Spirit, and absorb the atmosphere of centuries past. The Old Bridge connecting the two riverbanks offers stunning views of the cityscape.

Philosophers' Walk: For a panoramic perspective, embark on the Philosophers' Walk. This scenic path on the northern side of the Neckar River offers breathtaking views of Heidelberg, inspiring contemplation much like the philosophers who once ambled along its slopes.

Cultural Hub: Heidelberg is a cultural treasure trove, boasting an array of museums, galleries, and theatres. The Kurpfälzisches Museum and the Carl Bosch Museum provide insights into the city's history and contributions to science.

The Heidelberg Theatre adds a touch of the arts to your visit with its diverse performances.

Academic Legacy: Home to Germany's oldest University, Heidelberg University, founded in 1386, the city exudes an academic ambience. The University's Great Hall and Library are architectural marvels, reflecting centuries of intellectual pursuit.

Scenic Beauty along the Neckar River: Heidelberg's setting is enhanced by the meandering Neckar

River. A leisurely boat cruise or a romantic riverside walk unveils postcard-perfect scenes, with the castle looming above and the city's skyline reflecting in the tranquil waters.

Gastronomic Delights: Heidelberg's culinary scene is a fusion of traditional German flavours and international influences. From cosy beer gardens to fine dining establishments, the city invites you to savour delicious regional dishes and explore a vibrant cafe culture.

In essence, Heidelberg captivates with its blend of history, natural beauty, intellectual legacy, and cultural vibrancy. Whether you seek a romantic getaway, an exploration of history, or simply a serene retreat, Heidelberg awaits, promising an unforgettable travel experience.

Chapter Two

Getting To Heidelberg

Heidelberg's accessibility is key to its popularity as a travel destination. Here's a comprehensive guide to transportation options for reaching this enchanting city:

Transportation Options

Air Travel

- Frankfurt Airport (FRA): Situated approximately 80 kilometres from Heidelberg, Frankfurt Airport is a major international hub. Travelers can easily reach Heidelberg by taking direct trains or shuttle services from the airport to Heidelberg's central station.

- Stuttgart Airport (STR): Another viable option, Stuttgart Airport, is around 130 kilometres from

Heidelberg. Train services and shuttle buses connect the airport to Heidelberg, providing a convenient transfer for visitors.

Train Travel

- Heidelberg Hauptbahnhof: Heidelberg's main train station, Hauptbahnhof, is well-connected to major cities in Germany and neighbouring countries. High-speed trains, regional trains, and intercity services make Heidelberg easily accessible for rail travellers.

- ICE (InterCityExpress): Germany's high-speed rail network includes direct ICE connections to

Heidelberg from cities like Frankfurt, Munich, and Berlin, ensuring efficient and comfortable travel.

Car Rental

- Autobahns (Highways): Heidelberg is well-connected to Germany's autobahn network. Renting a car provides flexibility for those who prefer driving. The journey allows for picturesque views, especially when approaching Heidelberg through the Neckar Valley.

- Parking Facilities: The city offers various parking facilities, including street parking, parking garages, and park-and-ride options. Visitors should check specific parking regulations to ensure a hassle-free experience.

Bus Services

- Long-Distance Buses: Intercity bus services connect Heidelberg with various European cities. This cost-effective option is popular among budget-conscious travellers, offering comfortable rides and multiple drop-off points within the city.

Local Transportation

- Public Buses and Trams: Heidelberg boasts an efficient local transportation system with buses and trams covering the city and its surroundings. This is a convenient way to explore different neighbourhoods and attractions within Heidelberg.

Cycling

- Bike-Friendly City: Heidelberg's compact layout and well-maintained cycling paths make it a bike-friendly destination. Many visitors explore the city by bike, enjoying its scenic routes and flexibility.

Whether you prefer the speed of air travel, the convenience of train services, or the flexibility of driving, Heidelberg ensures a smooth and varied journey for every traveller.

Choose the transportation mode best suits your preferences and embark on an exciting journey to this historical and picturesque city.

Airport Information

For those arriving by air, Heidelberg is conveniently accessible through several airports. The primary airport serving the region is:

Frankfurt Airport (FRA)

Approximately 80 kilometres from Heidelberg, Frankfurt Airport is one of Europe's major international hubs. Travelers can easily reach Heidelberg from the airport by various transportation options:

- Train: The high-speed ICE trains connect Frankfurt Airport directly to Heidelberg's main station. The journey takes around 50-60 minutes, providing a comfortable and efficient way to travel.

- Shuttle Services: Airport shuttle and private transfers offer a convenient door-to-door option for travellers with heavy luggage or those seeking a more personalized experience.

- Rental Cars: Car rental services are available at the airport, providing flexibility for those who prefer driving. The journey to Heidelberg typically takes about an hour, depending on traffic.

Though further away, alternative airports include Stuttgart Airport (STR) and Baden Airpark (FKB). These airports also offer transportation options to Heidelberg, including train services and car rentals.

Stuttgart Airport (STR)

Located approximately 150 kilometres from Heidelberg, Stuttgart Airport provides an alternative gateway. Travelers can reach Heidelberg by train, car, or shuttle services.

Baden Airpark (FKB)

Situated about 100 kilometres away, Baden Airpark is a smaller airport serving the region. Travellers can use train connections or rental cars to reach Heidelberg from Baden Airpark.

Regardless of the chosen airport, the efficient German transportation network ensures a smooth journey to Heidelberg, allowing visitors to start their exploration of this captivating city with ease.

Local Public Transportation

Trains: Heidelberg boasts excellent rail connectivity, making it easily accessible from major German cities and neighbouring countries.

The Hauptbahnhof (Main Station) is a transportation hub, served by regular Intercity Express (ICE) and Regional Express (RE) trains. The efficient train network ensures a comfortable and scenic journey to and from Heidelberg.

Buses and Trams: Heidelberg's well-organized public transportation system includes an extensive network of buses and trams operated by the Rhein-Neckar-Verkehr (RNVP) company. These provide convenient and affordable means to explore the city and its surroundings. The efficient tram lines connect key points, offering a hassle-free way to move around Heidelberg.

HeidelbergCARD: For visitors planning to use public transportation extensively, the HeidelbergCARD is a valuable option. This card grants unlimited access to buses and trams and discounts on admission to various attractions. It's a cost-effective solution for those exploring the city's cultural and historical sites.

Biking: Heidelberg is a bicycle-friendly city with well-maintained bike paths. Many locals and tourists alike prefer exploring the city on two wheels. Numerous bike rental shops offer a convenient way to experience Heidelberg leisurely while enjoying the scenic surroundings.

Walking: Heidelberg's compact size and pedestrian-friendly layout make walking an enjoyable mode of transportation. The city's enchanting Old Town, castle, and riverside areas are best explored on foot, allowing you to immerse yourself in the ambience and discover hidden gems.

Taxi and Ride-Sharing: Taxis are readily available throughout the city, providing a convenient option for those seeking a more private and direct mode of transportation. Additionally, ride-sharing services

offer a modern and efficient way to move around Heidelberg.

With these diverse transportation options, getting around Heidelberg is convenient and an integral part of the experience, allowing you to appreciate the city's beauty and charm from various perspectives.

Chapter Three

Accommodation

Regarding accommodation in Heidelberg, the city offers a diverse range of options to suit every traveller's preferences.

From historic hotels to modern boutique stays, here's a detailed look at hotels in Heidelberg:

Hotels in Heidelberg

Heidelberg Marriott Hotel: Situated along the Neckar River, the Heidelberg Marriott Hotel combines modern luxury with breathtaking views of the city and castle.

It provides a comfortable and upscale stay with spacious rooms, an on-site spa, and a rooftop terrace.

Hotel Europäischer Hof Heidelberg: This five-star hotel, located near the Hauptbahnhof, boasts a rich history dating back to 1865. The Europäischer Hof blends tradition with modern amenities, offering guests elegantly appointed rooms, a spa, and multiple dining options.

Boutique Hotel Heidelberg Suites: This boutique hotel is a gem for those seeking a more intimate and stylish experience. Located on the banks of the Neckar River, it offers individually designed suites, personalized service, and a tranquil atmosphere.

Hotel Zum Ritter St. Georg: Nestled in the heart of Heidelberg's Old Town, this historic hotel dates back to the 16th century.

The Zum Ritter St. Georg exudes charm with its timber-framed facade and antique furnishings. Its central location makes it ideal for exploring the city's landmarks.

Leonardo Hotel Heidelberg: With a contemporary design, the Leonardo Hotel provides a comfortable and modern stay. Located near the Old Town, it offers easy access to major attractions. Amenities include a fitness centre, on-site dining, and well-appointed rooms.

Hotel Holländer Hof: This family-run hotel, located close to the Neckar River, offers a cosy and welcoming atmosphere.

The Holländer Hof features individually decorated rooms, a garden terrace, and a focus on personalized service, making guests feel at home.

Qube Heidelberg: A chic and eco-friendly option, Qube Heidelberg is known for its sustainable practices. The hotel's sleek design, innovative architecture, and commitment to environmental responsibility appeal to modern travellers seeking a mindful stay.

Whether you prefer a luxurious experience, a historic ambience, or a contemporary retreat, Heidelberg's hotels cater to various tastes and ensure a delightful stay while you explore the city's wonders.

Budget Accommodations

Hostels: Heidelberg has a selection of well-maintained hostels catering to budget-conscious travellers.

These hostels often provide dormitory-style accommodations with shared facilities, creating a social atmosphere for guests. Look for options near the city centre for easy access to key attractions.

Guesthouses and Pensions: Quaint guesthouses and pensions offer a more personalized experience while keeping costs in check. These family-run establishments often provide cosy rooms and a warm atmosphere, immersing guests in the local culture.

Short-Term Rentals: Platforms like Airbnb offer a range of affordable short-term rentals in Heidelberg. This option provides the flexibility of having your own space, which is particularly beneficial for those travelling in groups or seeking a more independent experience. Look for centrally located apartments to maximize convenience.

Student Residences: During vacation periods, some university student residences in Heidelberg open their doors to travellers. These budget-friendly options may offer basic amenities and a communal atmosphere, perfect for those looking for a unique experience.

Online Booking Platforms: Utilize popular online booking platforms to find competitive rates and special deals on budget accommodations. These platforms often provide reviews and ratings, allowing you to make an informed decision based on fellow travellers' experiences.

Regardless of your budget, Heidelberg ensures affordable accommodation options abound, allowing you to focus on exploring the city's rich history, cultural offerings, and picturesque surroundings without compromising on a comfortable place to stay.

Unique Stays

Historic Boutique Hotels: Immerse yourself in Heidelberg's rich history by staying in a charming boutique hotel. Many of these establishments are housed in beautifully restored buildings with period furnishings, providing an intimate and personalized atmosphere.

From centuries-old inns to boutique hotels in the heart of the Old Town, these accommodations blend history and modern comfort.

Castle Accommodations: For an unparalleled experience, consider staying within the walls of Heidelberg Castle itself. Some parts of the castle have been transformed into luxurious hotels, allowing guests to enjoy a regal atmosphere with stunning views of the city below.

Wake up to the medieval charm surrounding you and savour the unique privilege of residing within a historic fortress.

Riverside Retreats: Heidelberg's picturesque setting along the Neckar River offers opportunities for unique stays in riverside accommodations. Imagine waking up to the gentle flow of the river and enjoying panoramic views from your room.

Whether it's a boutique hotel, a cosy bed and breakfast, or a charming guesthouse, these riverside retreats provide a tranquil escape within the city.Themed Bed and Breakfasts: Heidelberg hosts a variety of themed bed and breakfasts, each offering a distinctive ambience.

From literary-inspired lodgings to art-focused guesthouses, these unique stays cater to travellers seeking an immersive and themed experience.

It's a chance to combine your accommodation with a specific interest or passion, adding an extra layer of enjoyment to your stay.

Treehouse Retreats: Consider booking a treehouse accommodation for a touch of whimsy and a unique connection with nature.

Nestled in the surrounding hills, these elevated retreats provide a cosy and enchanting escape, allowing you to experience Heidelberg from a different perspective while enjoying the tranquillity of the wooded surroundings.

When seeking accommodations in Heidelberg, these unique stays offer more than just a place to rest; they provide an integral part of your overall travel experience, creating lasting memories in this captivating German city.

Chapter Four

Must-See Attractions

Discovering Heidelberg is an enchanting journey through historic sites, scenic landscapes, and vibrant cultural spaces. One of the city's most iconic landmarks is the majestic Heidelberg Castle, a must-visit for any traveller.

Heidelberg Castle

Historical Marvel:

Perched atop the Königstuhl hill, Heidelberg Castle is a testament to centuries of history. Dating back to the 13th century, the castle has witnessed the ebb and flow of time, surviving wars, lightning strikes, and evolving architectural styles. Visitors can explore its captivating ruins, wandering through the courtyards and halls that once hosted royal banquets and festivities.

Great Barrel and Pharmacy Museum

Don't take advantage of the Great Barrel, a colossal wine barrel with a capacity of 220,000 litres within the castle complex. The Heidelberg Castle Pharmacy, one of the oldest in Germany, is another intriguing attraction.

It showcases a fascinating collection of historical remedies and potions, providing insight into medieval healthcare practices.

Panoramic Views

The castle offers breathtaking panoramic views of Heidelberg and the Neckar River. The terraces provide an ideal vantage point to capture the city's skyline, the Old Town's red-roofed houses, and the lush surrounding hills.

Sunset visits are magical, casting a warm glow over the city below.

The Elizabeth Gate and Gardens

As you explore the castle grounds adorned with stunning sculptures, the Elizabeth Gate beckons you to discover the castle gardens. These meticulously landscaped gardens feature vibrant flowers, sculptures, and pathways, creating a serene oasis with captivating views of Heidelberg and the Neckar Valley.

Guided Tours and Events

Immerse yourself in the castle's rich history with guided tours that delve into its stories, legends, and architectural intricacies. Heidelberg Castle hosts various events, including concerts and theatrical performances, providing a unique way to experience the site's cultural significance.

Funicular Railway

You can take the historic funicular railway from the Old Town to reach the castle, offering a scenic journey up the hill. The railway provides a convenient mode of transportation and an opportunity to enjoy breathtaking views of Heidelberg as you ascend to the castle.

Heidelberg Castle is an enduring symbol of the city's grandeur and resilience. It invites visitors to retreat and immerse themselves in medieval splendour and captivating vistas.

Old Town (Altstadt)

Historical Charm: Heidelberg's Old Town, or Altstadt, is a captivating labyrinth of narrow cobblestone streets and squares, exuding an irresistible medieval charm.

Stroll through these well-preserved streets, and you'll be transported back in time, surrounded by stunning examples of baroque architecture, half-timbered houses, and picturesque market squares.

Marktplatz: At the heart of the Old Town lies the Marktplatz, a vibrant square surrounded by historic buildings. The Church of the Holy Spirit

(Heiliggeistkirche) presides over the square, its Gothic architecture adding to the area's timeless appeal. The Marktplatz is a central hub and a gathering place for locals and visitors alike.

Alte Brücke (Old Bridge): Connecting the Old Town with the opposite bank of the Neckar River, the Alte Brücke is a picturesque stone bridge adorned with a medieval gate tower. This iconic structure provides breathtaking views of the castle and the city, making it a popular spot for photos and a leisurely riverside stroll.

Hauptstraße (Main Street): Hauptstraße, Heidelberg's main pedestrian street, runs through the heart of the Old Town. Lined with shops, boutiques, and cafes, it invites visitors to explore its offerings. The street is a bustling shopping district and a vibrant showcase of the city's lively atmosphere.

Universitätsplatz (University Square): As home to Germany's oldest University, Heidelberg's Old Town features the Universitätsplatz, a square surrounded by historic buildings and the imposing University Library. It's a hub of academic activity and a perfect spot to appreciate the city's intellectual legacy.

Heiliggeistkirche (Church of the Holy Spirit): Dominating the skyline of the Old Town, the Church of the Holy Spirit is a masterpiece of Gothic architecture.

Its interior boasts intricate details, including the famous "Bibliothekssaal" (Library Hall) and stunning stained glass windows. The church is a religious site and a cultural and historical landmark.

Exploring Heidelberg's Old Town is like stepping into a storybook, where every corner reveals a piece of the city's past.

From the lively market squares to the historic landmarks, the Altstadt is a must-visit destination that captures the essence of Heidelberg's timeless beauty.

Philosophers' Walk

Overview: The Philosophers' Walk, known locally as "Philosophenweg," is a scenic path on the Neckar River's northern side. This picturesque route has been a source of inspiration for philosophers, poets, and thinkers for centuries.

It offers captivating panoramic views of Heidelberg's Old Town, the castle, and the Neckar

River, creating a serene and contemplative atmosphere.

Historical Significance: The name "Philosophers' Walk" originates from the university professors and philosophers who frequented the path during the Romantic period.

It is said that these intellectuals used the tranquil setting to engage in reflective discussions and contemplation, drawing inspiration from the stunning vistas that unfold along the route.

Scenic Beauty: The walk starts near the Old Bridge and meanders through lush vineyards and terraced gardens. As you ascend the hill, you'll be treated to stunning views of Heidelberg's skyline, the castle perched atop the mountain, and the winding Neckar River below. The changing seasons add a layer of beauty, making it a delightful year-round experience.

Sites Along the Way: Along the Philosophers' Walk, you'll encounter points of interest such as the famous "Felsenmeer" (Sea of Rocks) and the Botanical Garden. The Felsenmeer is a collection of large, moss-covered stones, creating a unique and almost mystical atmosphere.

The Botanical Garden, established in 1593, showcases a diverse collection of plant species and adds to the natural allure of the walk.

Hiking and Recreation: Beyond its historical and scenic appeal, the Philosophers' Walk provides an excellent opportunity for outdoor enthusiasts. The well-maintained path is suitable for a stroll or a more vigorous hike, depending on your preferences. The tranquillity of the surroundings makes it an ideal escape for those seeking a break from the bustling city below.

Sunset Views: The Philosophers' Walk is enchanting during sunset, as the fading sunlight bathes Heidelberg in warm hues. This magical moment adds a touch of romance to an already captivating experience, making it a popular spot for couples and photographers alike.

In essence, the Philosophers' Walk is a journey through nature and history, inviting visitors to slow down, reflect, and appreciate the timeless beauty of Heidelberg from a vantage point that has inspired generations of thinkers.

Neckar River Cruise

Overview: Embarking on a Neckar River Cruise offers a leisurely and scenic journey, allowing you to appreciate Heidelberg's beauty from the tranquil waters of the Neckar River. Whether you're a nature enthusiast, a history buff, or seeking a romantic experience, the river cruise promises a delightful adventure.

Sailing Through History: As you glide along the river, you'll be treated to panoramic views of Heidelberg's skyline, dominated by the iconic Heidelberg Castle perched on the hills. With its medieval charm, the castle becomes even more enchanting when viewed from the water. Your cruise provides a unique vantage point, allowing you to capture stunning photographs of this architectural masterpiece.

Romantic Ambiance: The Neckar River Cruise is renowned for its romantic ambience, making it an ideal activity for couples.

The gentle movement of the boat, the reflections of city lights on the water, and the picturesque landscapes create a captivating atmosphere. Sunset cruises, in particular, offer a magical experience as the fading sunlight bathes Heidelberg in warm hues.

Guided Narration: Many river cruises offer guided narrations, providing insights into the history and culture of Heidelberg.

Learn fascinating anecdotes about the landmarks you pass, the role of the river in the city's development, and the legends associated with the surrounding landscapes. This educational aspect enhances your appreciation of the town and its surroundings.

Lush Riverside Scenery: The Neckar River is bordered by lush greenery and charming villages, adding to the visual appeal of the cruise. The natural beauty along the riverbanks creates a serene backdrop, inviting you to relax and unwind as you soak in the tranquillity of the surroundings.

Accessibility: River cruises are easily accessible, with departure points conveniently located along the river in Heidelberg. Whether you opt for a short daytime cruise or a romantic evening journey, the experience suits visitors of all ages and interests.In conclusion, a Neckar River Cruise in Heidelberg is not merely a boat ride; it's a captivating journey

through history, nature, and romance. It provides a refreshing perspective on the city's landmarks and landscapes, ensuring an unforgettable addition to your Heidelberg adventure.

Chapter Five

Dining and Cuisine

One of the highlights of visiting Heidelberg is indulging in its diverse culinary scene. When it comes to savouring the authentic flavours of the region, Traditional German Cuisine takes centre stage.

Traditional German Cuisine

Hearty Delights: Traditional German cuisine is celebrated for its hearty and flavorful dishes. In Heidelberg, you can relish classics such as "Sauerbraten" (marinated pot roast), "Schweinshaxe" (roasted pork knuckle), and "Bratwurst" (grilled sausage). These dishes, often accompanied by rich sauces and savoury sides, exemplify German gastronomy's robust and satisfying nature.

Bavarian Influence: Heidelberg's proximity to Bavaria contributes to the city's vibrant culinary offerings. Expect to find Bavarian specialities like "Pretzels" with mustard, "Weisswurst" (white sausage), and "Obatzda" (a creamy cheese spread). Pair these with a locally brewed beer for an authentic taste of the region.

Beer Gardens and Halls: To fully immerse yourself in the German dining experience, visit one of Heidelberg's traditional beer gardens or halls.

These venues not only serve a variety of local and regional beers but also offer an extensive menu featuring classic German fare. Enjoy your meal in a convivial atmosphere surrounded by locals and fellow travellers.

Wine Culture: While beer is a prominent feature, Heidelberg's location in the Baden wine region means wine enthusiasts have plenty to celebrate. Explore the city's wine taverns, known as "Weinstuben," to sample regional wines like Riesling and Spätburgunder. Many restaurants also incorporate local wines into their menus, providing a delightful complement to traditional dishes.

Desserts and Pastries: No exploration of German cuisine is complete without indulging in delightful desserts. Treat yourself to "Black Forest Cake" (Schwarzwälder Kirschtorte), apple strudel, or a warm "Bienenstich" (bee sting cake) at one of Heidelberg's charming cafés or pastry shops.

Local Markets: For an authentic culinary adventure, visit Heidelberg's markets. The Hauptstraße, the city's main street, often hosts food markets where you can taste regional specialities and purchase fresh produce. Don't miss the opportunity to try local cheeses, bread, and artisanal products.

Whether savouring a traditional meal in a cosy Gasthaus or exploring the culinary delights at a lively beer garden, Traditional German Cuisine in Heidelberg promises a gastronomic journey that captures the the essence of the rich culinary history of the area.

Local Restaurants and Cafés

Zum Güldenen Schaf (The Golden Sheep): Nestled in Heidelberg's Old Town, Zum Güldenen Schaf is a historic restaurant with a cosy atmosphere. Known for its traditional German dishes, this establishment offers a menu featuring regional specialities like Schnitzel and Sauerbraten. The rustic ambience and warm hospitality make it a favourite among locals and visitors.

Destille: For a taste of local Heidelberg brews and hearty German cuisine, Destille is a popular choice. This tavern-style restaurant provides a laid-back setting to enjoy dishes such as Flammkuchen (a thin-crust pizza) and a variety of sausages. The extensive beer selection, including regional brews, adds to the authentic experience.

Hackteufel: Situated in the heart of the Old Town, Hackteufel is a charming restaurant offering traditional and modern dishes. Its timber-framed facade and welcoming interiors provide an inviting space to relish German classics like Rouladen and Käsespätzle.

The restaurant's commitment to using fresh, locally sourced ingredients enhances the quality of the dining experience.

Café Knösel: For a delightful coffee break or a sweet treat, Café Knösel is a renowned café in Heidelberg.

Established in 1889, this historic café exudes old-world charm.

Indulge in freshly baked pastries, cakes, and artisanal chocolates while enjoying the elegant ambience. The outdoor terrace offers a perfect spot to unwind and people-watch in the lively Hauptstraße.

Vetter's Alt Heidelberger Brauhaus: Beer enthusiasts should take advantage of Vetter's, home to one of the strongest beers globally, the Vetter 33. This traditional brewpub serves up hearty German fare alongside its famous brews.

The rustic setting, complete with wooden beams and copper brewing kettles, creates a cosy atmosphere for a memorable dining experience.

Marktplatz Restaurants: Heidelberg's Marktplatz is adorned with charming restaurants and cafés offering local and international cuisines. This central square is an excellent place to explore culinary diversity, from authentic German dishes to

Mediterranean flavours. Outdoor seating allows you to enjoy your meal while soaking in the vibrant atmosphere of the Old Town.

In Heidelberg, dining is not just a necessity; it's an integral part of the cultural experience.

These local restaurants and cafés showcase the city's diverse culinary scene, inviting you to embark on a gastronomic journey that reflects Heidelberg and Germany's rich flavours and traditions.

Popular Dishes to Try

Sauerbraten: A quintessential German dish, Sauerbraten is a pot roast, usually of beef, marinated in vinegar, water, and a medley of spices. The marinated meat is slow-cooked to perfection, resulting in a tender and flavorful dish.

Served with red cabbage and potato dumplings (Kartoffelklöße), Sauerbraten showcases German cuisine's hearty and savoury side.

Spätzle: This Swabian egg noodle dish is a culinary delight in Germany, and Heidelberg is no exception. Spätzle is often served as a side dish or the main attraction, accompanied by rich sauces, cheese, or topped with crispy onions. Its soft, chewy texture makes it a comforting and versatile choice.

Flammkuchen: Often referred to as "German pizza," is a thin, crispy crust topped with crème fraîche, onions, and bacon.

This Alsatian speciality has found its way into German cuisine and is a popular choice in Heidelberg. Combining smoky bacon and creamy

crème fraîche creates a harmonious and delicious flavour profile.

Käsespätzle: A savoury treat for cheese lovers, Käsespätzle is a comforting dish that features Spätzle noodles mixed with melted cheese, often Emmental or Gruyère. This hearty dish is baked perfectly, creating a golden crust. It's a favourite comfort food, offering a rich and indulgent experience.

Weißwurst with Pretzel: Embrace the Bavarian influence with Weißwurst, a traditional white sausage made from minced veal and pork back bacon. Typically flavoured with parsley, mace, onions, ginger, and cardamom, Weißwurst is served with sweet mustard and freshly baked pretzels. It's a flavorful and iconic dish often enjoyed as a mid-morning snack or light lunch.

Apfelstrudel: No culinary journey is complete without a sweet ending, and Apfelstrudel is a beloved dessert in Heidelberg. This apple strudel features thin layers of pastry filled with spiced apples, raisins, and nuts. Served warm and dusted with powdered sugar, it's a delightful treat that perfectly captures the essence of German baking.

As you explore the dining scene in Heidelberg, these popular dishes provide a delicious introduction to the city's culinary heritage. Each bite is a flavorful journey through the traditions and tastes that make Heidelberg's cuisine a memorable experience.

Chapter Six

Shopping in Heidelberg

Heidelberg's shopping scene is a delightful blend of historic markets and trendy boutiques, offering diverse products that reflect the city's rich cultural heritage. Explore the following markets and boutiques for a unique shopping experience:

Markets and Boutiques

Marktplatz (Market Square): The heart of Heidelberg's shopping district is surrounded by charming boutiques and stores.

You can find everything from local crafts and souvenirs to fresh produce and flowers here. The Market Square is a shopping destination and a cultural hub where street performers and events often occur.

Altstadt Boutiques: Heidelberg's Old Town (Altstadt) is a treasure trove of boutiques that cater to diverse tastes. Wander through the cobblestone streets to discover unique fashion, accessories, and handmade items. From designer boutiques to quaint shops, the Old Town offers a curated selection of goods reflecting tradition and modernity.

Heidelberg Hauptstraße: As one of Europe's longest pedestrian streets, Hauptstraße is a shopper's paradise. The street has many boutiques, international brands, and speciality stores. Whether looking for fashion, jewellery, or speciality items, Hauptstraße has something for every shopper.

Heidelberger Herbst (Heidelberg Autumn): This annual fall market is a must-visit for those interested in unique arts and crafts. Heidelberger Herbst transforms the Old Town into a lively market showcasing handmade products, local art, and regional delicacies. It's an excellent opportunity to support local artisans and find one-of-a-kind souvenirs.

Antique Shops in Neuenheim: The Neuenheim district, located on the northern bank of the Neckar River, is known for its antique shops. Antique enthusiasts can explore these establishments to discover vintage furniture, rare books, and unique collectables. It's a charming area for those seeking timeless pieces with a touch of history.

Heidelberg Christmas Market: If your visit coincides with the holiday season, the Heidelberg Christmas Market is a magical experience.

Held in the Old Town, this market features festive stalls selling handcrafted ornaments, seasonal treats, and traditional gifts. The twinkling lights and lively atmosphere create a winter wonderland for shoppers.

Studentenkarzer Gift Shop: Located near the University, the Studentenkarzer (Student Prison) Gift Shop offers quirky and humorous souvenirs.

The Studentenkarzer was a real prison for naughty students in the past, and the gift shop reflects this history with a range of amusing and unique items.

Heidelberg's markets and boutiques provide a delightful mix of traditional and contemporary shopping experiences. Whether you are searching for handmade crafts, fashionable attire, or timeless antiques, Heidelberg invites you to explore its diverse shopping destinations.

Souvenirs from Heidelberg

Heidelberg Castle Memorabilia: Commemorate your visit to Heidelberg with souvenirs inspired by its iconic castle. Gift shops in and around the castle offer a variety of items, including miniature replicas, postcards, and decorative pieces. Whether it's a keychain or a detailed model, these souvenirs capture the majesty of Heidelberg Castle.

Studentenkarzer Memorabilia: Dive into Heidelberg's university culture with souvenirs from the Studentenkarzer, the historical student prison. Pick up quirky items like mugs, T-shirts, or posters adorned with humorous illustrations and slogans reflecting the unique traditions of Heidelberg University.

Old Town Keepsakes: Explore the charming streets of Heidelberg's Old Town, where you'll find an array of boutiques and gift shops. Look for locally crafted items such as handmade jewellery, traditional German crafts, and unique accessories. These one-of-a-kind keepsakes capture the essence of the city's historic ambience.

Philosophers' Walk-inspired Art: The Philosophers' Walk, with its stunning views of Heidelberg, inspires many local artists. Seek out art galleries or craft markets for paintings, prints, or photography to capture the beauty of this iconic spot. Bringing home a piece of art allows you to carry the picturesque landscapes of Heidelberg with you.

Beer Steins and Glassware: Embrace Heidelberg's beer culture by purchasing a traditional German beer stein or a set of locally crafted glassware. These items often feature intricate designs and can be found in speciality shops or at the Heidelberg Christmas Market if visiting during the festive season.

Heidelberg Literature and Poetry Books: Heidelberg has a rich literary history, with famous poets like Goethe drawing inspiration from the city. Explore local bookshops for literature and poetry collections associated with Heidelberg. A beautifully bound edition of classic works or contemporary writings inspired by the city makes for a thoughtful souvenir.

Hauptstraße Fashion Finds: Hauptstraße, Heidelberg's main shopping street, offers a mix of high-end fashion and quirky boutiques. Discover stylish clothing, accessories, and unique fashion pieces to bring a touch of Heidelberg's trendy side back home.

Local Food and Wine: Culinary enthusiasts will appreciate bringing back local flavours. Look for speciality shops offering Heidelberg's unique food products, such as mustard, chocolates, and regional wines. A bottle of local wine or a box of handmade chocolates makes a delicious reminder of your time in Heidelberg.

Heidelberg's souvenir options cater to various tastes, allowing you to find the perfect souvenir that resonates with your experience in this picturesque city. Whether it's a piece of history, artistic inspiration, or a culinary delight,

Heidelberg's souvenir offerings are as diverse as its cultural tapestry.

Chapter Seven

Cultural Experiences

Immerse yourself in Heidelberg's rich cultural tapestry by exploring its museums and galleries. From historical artefacts to contemporary art, the city offers diverse cultural experiences for enthusiasts of all interests.

Museums and Galleries

Heidelberg Castle Museum: Begin your cultural journey at the Heidelberg Castle, home to the Heidelberg Castle Museum (Schlossmuseum).

This museum traces the city's history from the medieval period to today. Explore the castle's interiors, filled with artefacts, paintings, and interactive exhibits that vividly narrate the stories of royalty, battles, and daily life in Heidelberg.

Kurpfälzisches Museum: Located in the heart of Heidelberg's Old Town, the Kurpfälzisches Museum is a treasure trove of art and artefacts.

The museum showcases a diverse collection, including paintings, sculptures, and applied arts, providing insight into the region's cultural development. The museum comprehensively views Heidelberg's artistic heritage, from Renaissance masterpieces to contemporary works.

Carl Bosch Museum: Science enthusiasts will appreciate a visit to the Carl Bosch Museum. Dedicated to the life and work of Nobel laureate and chemist Carl Bosch, this museum explores the history of chemical engineering.

Discover the innovations that shaped the chemical industry and learn about Bosch's contributions to science and technology.

Deutsches Apotheken-Museum (German Pharmacy Museum): Housed within Heidelberg Castle, this unique museum transports visitors to the fascinating history of pharmacy and medicine. The collection includes antique pharmaceutical instruments, medicinal herbs, and apothecary jars, offering a captivating glimpse into the evolution of healthcare practices.

Art Galleries in Heidelberg: The city boasts a vibrant art scene, with numerous galleries showcasing a variety of artistic expressions.

Explore contemporary art spaces like the Kunstverein Heidelberg or visit galleries along Hauptstraße featuring works by local and international artists. The blend of traditional and modern art reflects Heidelberg's dynamic cultural landscape.

University Museum: Heidelberg's long-standing academic legacy is celebrated at the University Museum. Located within Heidelberg University, this museum delves into the institution's history, highlighting milestones, influential figures, and academic achievements. It provides a fascinating perspective on the intellectual contributions that have emanated from Heidelberg over the centuries.

Palatinate Museum of Natural History: Nature enthusiasts can explore the Palatinate Museum of Natural History (Pfalzmuseum für Naturkunde). This museum, located in Heidelberg's Neuenheim district, showcases the region's flora and fauna through exhibits on geology, palaeontology, and local ecosystems.

Whether you're drawn to history, art, science, or natural wonders, Heidelberg's museums and galleries offer rich cultural experiences.

Each institution contributes to the city's vibrant cultural mosaic, inviting visitors to delve into the stories, discoveries, and artistic expressions that have shaped Heidelberg's identity.

Theatres and Performing Arts

Heidelberg Theatre (Heidelberger Theater): Situated in the heart of the city, the Heidelberg Theatre is a cultural hub hosting diverse performances. From classical plays and contemporary dramas to musicals and dance productions, the theatre offers a dynamic program that caters to various tastes. The historic ambience of the venue enhances the overall theatrical experience.

Old Bridge Studios: For a more intimate setting, consider attending performances at Old Bridge Studios. This venue often showcases experimental and innovative works in theatre and performing arts. The focus on cutting-edge performances provides cultural enthusiasts with a unique and thought-provoking experience.

Street Performances in Old Town: Heidelberg's Old Town comes alive with spontaneous street performances. Talented artists, musicians, and performers bring their craft to the charming cobblestone streets, creating an immersive and interactive cultural experience. From classical melodies to contemporary dance, these impromptu performances add vibrancy to the city's atmosphere.

Jazzhaus Heidelberg: Jazz enthusiasts will find a haven at Jazzhaus Heidelberg. This intimate venue hosts live jazz performances featuring local and international artists. The cosy ambience and acoustics make it an ideal spot to enjoy an evening of soulful tunes and improvisation.

Festivals and Events

Heidelberger Frühling (Heidelberg Spring): This annual music festival transforms Heidelberg into celebrating classical music and contemporary compositions. Held in various venues across the city, Heidelberger Frühling attracts renowned musicians and emerging talents, offering a diverse program that includes concerts, masterclasses, and discussions.

Castle Illuminations: Experience the magic of Heidelberg Castle Illuminations, a spectacular event where the castle is illuminated with a play of lights and fireworks. This traditional event, held several times a year, attracts crowds to the banks of the Neckar River for an enchanting view of the illuminated castle against the night sky.

Christmas Market (Weihnachtsmarkt): Heidelberg's Christmas Market is a festive highlight, transforming the Old Town into a winter wonderland.

The market features charming stalls selling handmade crafts, seasonal treats, and festive decorations. Carol singers, the scent of mulled wine, and the twinkling lights create a magical atmosphere during the holiday season.

Heidelberg Literature Days (Heidelberger Literaturtage): For literature enthusiasts, the Heidelberg Literature Days offer a platform for authors, poets, and readers to come together. The event includes readings, discussions, and book presentations, fostering a literary dialogue in the city.

Cultural experiences in Heidelberg are not confined to historical landmarks; they extend to the theatres, performances, festivals, and events that showcase the city's dynamic and evolving artistic spirit.

Whether attending a classical concert, enjoying a street performance, or immersing yourself in a festive market, Heidelberg's cultural offerings promise memorable and enriching experiences.

Chapter Eight

Outdoor Activities

Heidelberg's scenic surroundings and diverse landscapes provide a perfect backdrop for outdoor activities. Whether you're a nature enthusiast, sports lover, or someone seeking leisurely recreation, Heidelberg offers a range of options to enjoy the great outdoors.

Hiking and Nature Trails

Philosophers' Walk (Philosophenweg): One of Heidelberg's most famous trails, the Philosophers' Walk, winds along the Neckar River and offers breathtaking city views.

Named after the philosophers and professors who frequented the path for contemplation, this trail is surrounded by lush greenery and provides a serene escape from the urban hustle. The panorama of

Heidelberg's Old Town and castle from the elevated path is truly picturesque.

Heiligenberg and Michaelskloster Trail: Explore the Heiligenberg, the "Holy Mountain," and discover the ruins of Michaelskloster, an ancient monastery.

The trail takes you through the forested hills, passing by remnants of historical structures and offering serene moments of tranquillity. It's an ideal route for those seeking a combination of nature and history.

Königstuhl Nature Reserve: Venture into the Königstuhl Nature Reserve on Heidelberg's highest hill. With a network of trails, you can explore the diverse flora and fauna while enjoying panoramic views of the city and surrounding landscapes.

Hiking through the lush forested paths provides a refreshing escape into nature.

Parks and Gardens

Botanischer Garten (Botanical Garden): Located near the Neuenheimer Feld, Heidelberg's Botanical Garden is a haven for plant enthusiasts. Explore themed sections such as alpine plants, medicinal herbs, and tropical greenhouses. The garden's diverse collection of flora makes it a delightful spot for education and relaxation.

Schlossgarten (Castle Garden): Adjacent to Heidelberg Castle, the Schlossgarten is a beautifully landscaped garden offering a peaceful retreat. Stroll through manicured lawns, enjoy blooming flowerbeds, and marvel at the views of the castle and Old Town. The garden provides a serene environment for a leisurely walk or a relaxing picnic.

Sports and Recreation

Neckar River Activities: The Neckar River offers opportunities for various water-based activities. Kayaking, canoeing, or taking a leisurely boat cruise are popular options. Paddle along the riverbanks to admire the cityscape or embark on a more adventurous journey downstream.

Cycling along the Neckar: Heidelberg's well-maintained cycling paths make it an ideal city for biking enthusiasts. Rent a bike, explore the scenic routes along the Neckar River, or venture into the surrounding hills. The gentle slopes and picturesque landscapes make cycling an enjoyable outdoor activity.

Golf at Golf Club Heidelberg-Lobenfeld: Golf enthusiasts can tee off at the Golf Club Heidelberg-Lobenfeld, situated in the hills surrounding Heidelberg. The club offers a challenging 18-hole course with panoramic views, providing a serene and sporty escape.

Heidelberg's outdoor activities cater to a wide range of interests, allowing residents and visitors alike to embrace nature, engage in physical activities, and appreciate the city's stunning landscapes. Whether hiking, strolling through gardens, or enjoying recreational sports, the outdoor offerings in Heidelberg are diverse and inviting.

Chapter Nine

Practical Tips

Heidelberg, with its blend of history and modernity, offers a welcoming experience for visitors. Here are practical tips to enhance your stay in this charming German city.

Weather and Best Time to Visit

Weather Overview: Heidelberg experiences a temperate oceanic climate with four seasons. Summers (June to August) are generally mild to warm, while winters (December to February) can be cold with occasional snow.

Spring (March to May) and autumn (September to November) are pleasant times to visit, with milder temperatures and colourful landscapes.

Best Time to Visit: The spring and fall months are considered the best times to visit Heidelberg. The weather is typically comfortable during these periods, and the city is adorned with blooming flowers or autumn foliage.

Summer is also popular, but it can be busier with tourists. Winter, although festive with Christmas markets, is colder and less crowded.

Local Customs and Etiquette

Greeting: Germans often greet with a handshake, accompanied by a polite "Guten Tag" (Good day) or "Hallo." Friends and acquaintances may exchange cheek kisses.

Politeness: Germans appreciate politeness and consider it important in social interactions. Saying "Bitte" (please) and "Danke" (thank you) goes a long way in showing respect.

Tipping: Service charges are usually included in restaurant bills, but leaving small changes or rounding up the bill is customary. In cafés, rounding up is also common. Tipping taxi drivers and hotel staff is familiar.

Quiet Sundays: Sundays are generally quiet in Germany, with many shops closed. It's a day to kick back and spend with loved ones. Plan accordingly and check for open restaurants and attractions.

Safety Information

General Safety: Heidelberg is a safe city for visitors. However, it's advisable to practice general safety precautions. Keep an eye on your belongings, especially in crowded areas, and be cautious with personal valuables.

Healthcare: Medical facilities in Heidelberg are of a high standard. The city has well-equipped hospitals and pharmacies. EU citizens with a European Health

Insurance Card (EHIC) may be eligible for medical services.

Emergency Services: In emergencies, dial 112 for medical assistance, fire, or police. The emergency services in Heidelberg are efficient and responsive.

Public Transportation Safety: Heidelberg's public transportation is safe and reliable. Be aware of the schedules, especially for trains and buses, and follow standard safety guidelines when using public transport.

Heidelberg's welcoming atmosphere and efficient infrastructure make it an enjoyable destination. By being mindful of local customs, staying informed about the weather, and practising general safety measures, you can make the most of your visit to this picturesque city.

Chapter Ten

Day Trips from Heidelberg

Heidelberg's strategic location in the heart of the Rhine-Neckar region opens up many exciting day-trip options. Explore the nearby towns and attractions to enrich your Heidelberg experience. One notable day-trip destination is:

Schwetzingen Palace

Overview: Located just a short distance from Heidelberg, Schwetzingen Palace is a remarkable example of Baroque architecture and landscape design.

This enchanting palace complex, surrounded by extensive gardens, offers a glimpse into the elegance and grandeur of 18th-century Germany.

Palace and Gardens: Schwetzingen Palace is renowned for its beautifully landscaped gardens, featuring meticulously designed flowerbeds, water elements, and sculptures.

The palace boasts opulent interiors with stunning frescoes, lavish furnishings, and ornate decorations. Explore the various wings, halls, and chambers that showcase the artistic and architectural achievements of the time.

Temple of Apollo: One of the highlights of the palace grounds is the Temple of Apollo. This classical structure, surrounded by water, is a stunning focal point in the gardens. The serene atmosphere and picturesque setting make it a perfect spot for reflecting and appreciating the Baroque aesthetic.

Historic Theater: Schwetzingen Palace is home to a charming Rococo theatre that has been meticulously preserved. The theatre hosts regular performances, providing a unique opportunity to experience classical music and drama in an authentic 18th-century setting.

Festivals and Events: Schwetzingen Palace hosts various cultural events and festivals annually. The most notable is the Schwetzingen Festival, which celebrates classical music and opera. Attending one of these events during your day trip can add a cultural dimension to your experience.

How to Get There: Schwetzingen is conveniently accessible by train or car from Heidelberg. The train journey takes approximately 20 minutes, and the palace is a short walk from the Schwetzingen train station. If driving, it's about a 15-minute journey via the A5 highway.

Practical Tips: Check the palace's official website for information on guided tours, events, and opening hours. Consider combining your visit with a stroll through the charming town of Schwetzingen, known for its picturesque streets and local eateries.

A day trip to Schwetzingen Palace offers a captivating blend of history, art, and natural beauty. The palace and its grounds provide a tranquil escape, allowing you to immerse yourself in the elegance of the Baroque era just a short distance from Heidelberg.

Speyer Cathedral

Overview: Located approximately an hour's drive south of Heidelberg, Speyer Cathedral, or Speyerer Dom, stands as a UNESCO World Heritage Site and a masterpiece of Romanesque architecture. This majestic cathedral symbolizes Speyer's historical significance and cultural heritage.

Architectural Marvel: Speyer Cathedral, consecrated in 1061, is a remarkable example of Romanesque architecture.

The cathedral's red sandstone exterior is adorned with intricate sculptures and carvings, showcasing the craftsmanship of its builders. The imposing structure dominates the skyline of Speyer and is visible from a distance as you approach the city.

Imperial Cathedral: The cathedral served as the burial site for German emperors for centuries, making it one of the most important imperial cathedrals in the country. The tombs of emperors and kings, including that of Emperor Rudolf II, add a historical and regal dimension to the cathedral's significance.

Historical Significance: Speyer Cathedral has withstood the test of time, surviving wars and renovations. It serves as a testament to medieval builders' resilience and architectural prowess.

The interior features a grand nave, intricately designed columns, and stunning stained glass windows, creating an awe-inspiring atmosphere for visitors.

Climbing the Tower: Adventurous visitors can climb the tower for panoramic views of Speyer and its surroundings. The ascent provides a unique perspective on the cathedral's architecture and offers breathtaking vistas of the city and the Rhine River.

Surrounding Area: Speyer is a charming town with a picturesque Old Town, quaint streets, and historical buildings. After exploring the cathedral, wander through the streets to discover the Altpörtel, a medieval gate tower, and the Jewish courtyard, which reflects Speyer's rich cultural diversity.

Transportation: Speyer is easily accessible from Heidelberg by car or public transportation. The train journey takes approximately one hour, and from the Speyer train station, it's a short walk to the cathedral and the town centre.

A day trip to Speyer Cathedral from Heidelberg promises architectural marvels and a journey through centuries of history.

Immerse yourself in the grandeur of this UNESCO-listed cathedral, explore Speyer's charming town, and appreciate the cultural heritage that enriches the Rhine-Neckar region.

Mannheim Water Tower

Overview: The Mannheim Water Tower, locally known as "Wasserturm," is an architectural gem and a symbol of Mannheim's history. This stunning structure is a functional water reservoir and a captivating monument at the heart of Friedrichsplatz, one of the city's central squares.

Architectural Marvel: Erected between 1886 and 1889, the Mannheim Water Tower boasts an impressive neoclassical design. Designed by Gustav Halmhuber, the tower stands 60 meters (197 feet) tall and is crowned with a dome. Its architecture is characterized by a harmonious blend of Renaissance and Art Nouveau elements, making it a distinctive and aesthetically pleasing landmark.

Friedrichsplatz Gardens: Surrounding the Mannheim Water Tower is the scenic Friedrichsplatz Gardens. These well-maintained green spaces offer a tranquil setting for a stroll or a relaxing afternoon picnic. Combining the elegant water tower and the picturesque gardens creates a charming ambience.

Observation Deck: The Mannheim Water Tower features an observation deck that provides panoramic views of Mannheim and the surrounding region. Climbing to the top allows visitors to appreciate the city's layout, the Neckar River, and even glimpses of the Odenwald forest in the distance. It's a perfect vantage point for capturing memorable photographs.

Cultural Hub: Friedrichsplatz is a cultural hub with a water tower. The square hosts events, festivals, and open-air concerts throughout the year. The Water Tower Festival, in particular, is a highlight that attracts locals and visitors, adding a lively and festive atmosphere to the surroundings.

City Center Accessibility: The Mannheim Water Tower is conveniently located in Mannheim's city centre, making it easily accessible from Heidelberg. A short train or car ride brings you to this architectural marvel, allowing for a delightful day trip that combines cultural exploration with leisurely walks in the adjacent gardens.

When considering day trips from Heidelberg, visiting the Mannheim Water Tower offers a perfect blend of history, architecture, and scenic beauty.

Whether you're interested in the cultural events at Friedrichsplatz or want to enjoy panoramic views from the observation deck, this excursion promises a memorable experience.

Conclusion

In conclusion, Heidelberg is a captivating destination that blends history, culture, and natural beauty. This travel guide has aimed to provide a comprehensive overview, offering insights into the city's historic landmarks, cultural experiences, outdoor activities, and practical tips for a memorable visit.

From the iconic Heidelberg Castle overlooking the Old Town to the serene Neckar River and the enchanting Philosophers' Walk, the city unfolds a tapestry of experiences for every traveller. The local cuisine, festivals, and theatres contribute to the vibrant cultural scene, while outdoor enthusiasts can explore scenic trails, parks, and recreational activities.

As you navigate Heidelberg's charming streets, indulge in its culinary delights, and immerse yourself in its rich cultural offerings, may this travel guide serve as a companion, unlocking the wonders and hidden gems of this picturesque German city. Whether you seek history, nature, or vibrant city life, Heidelberg welcomes you with open arms, inviting you to explore its timeless charm and create lasting memories. Safe travels!

Printed in Great Britain
by Amazon

43493654R00059